ONE NATION FOR ALL
IMMIGRANTS IN THE UNITED STATES

LIFE AS A SOMALI AMERICAN

ELLEN CREAGER

PowerKiDS
press™

Published in 2018 by The Rosen Publishing Group, Inc.
29 East 21st Street, New York, NY 10010

Cataloging-in-Publication Data

Names: Creager, Ellen.
Title: Life as a Somali American / Ellen Creager.
Description: New York : PowerKids Press, 2018. | Series: One nation for all: immigrants in the United States | Includes index.
Identifiers: LCCN ISBN 9781538323427 (pbk.) | ISBN 9781538322468 (library bound) | ISBN 9781538323434 (6 pack)
Subjects: LCSH: Somali Americans--Juvenile literature. | Immigrants--United States-- Juvenile literature.
Classification: LCC E184.S67 C74 2018 | DDC 973'.0496773--dc23

Developed and produced for Rosen by BlueApple*Works* Inc.
Art Director: T.J. Choleva
Managing Editor for BlueApple*Works*: Melissa McClellan
Designer: Joshua Avramson
Photo Research: Jane Reid
Editor: Marcia Abramson

Photo Credits: cover Vladgalenko/Dreamstime.com; title page photo.ua/Shutterstock.com; flag Les Cunliffe/ Dreamstime; background HorenkO/Shutterstock; p. 4 Adrian Sherratt/Alamy Stock Photo; p. 8 Serban Bogdan/ Shutterstock; p. 11 inset AMISOM Public Information/Creative Commons; p. 11 Petty Officer 2nd Class Daniel Barker, U.S. Navy/Public Domain; p. 12 hikrcn/Shutterstock.com; p. 14 Vladgalenko/Dreamstime.com; p. 17 Benny Marty/Shutterstock.com; p. 18 Alf Ribeiro/Shutterstock.com; p. 20 left, 24 Free Wind 2014/Shutterstock.com; p. 20 T. Choleva; p. 22 Jenny Matthews/Alamy Stock Photo; p. 26 Lorie Shaull; p. 29 Featureflash Photo Agency/ Shutterstock.com

Manufactured in the United States of America
CPSIA Compliance Information: Batch BW18PK: For Further Information contact
Rosen Publishing, New York, New York at 1-800-237-9932.

CONTENTS

U.S. families with roots in the country of Somalia are known as Somali Americans.

WHO ARE SOMALI AMERICANS?

Most Somali immigrants have arrived in the United States since the 1990s. They are becoming an integral part of communities across the country. Many Somali Americans live in the state of Minnesota, where it is easy to find a Somali restaurant, **mosque**, shop, or even a mall. Ilhan Omar, the nation's first Somali American to be elected to political office, is also from Minnesota.

Many Somali Americans have made their homes in Columbus, Ohio; Lewiston and Portland, Maine; and Seattle, Washington. An estimated 145,000 Somali Americans live in the United States, according to 2015 census data. Early arrivals came for jobs or education. Recent arrivals have come as refugees fleeing civil war and trouble in Somalia.

Somali immigrants may attend night school to learn about their new country.

Somali is the most spoken language in Somalia, followed by Arabic. Many Somali immigrants are unfamiliar with English when they arrive in the United States. This can make it difficult for Somali Americans to find jobs. They may take classes to learn English.

Somali American Fashion

Dirac: Women's long dresses made of brightly colored fabric, often with patterns and weaves.

Garbasaar: Long shawl often worn with matching dirac.

Masar: Scarf.

Hijab: Scarf that completely covers the hair. Some Somali women also use the word hijab for garments that give even greater covering of the head and body. Somali American women's clothing does not cover their faces.

Shuka: Long overcoat.

Macawiis: In Somalia, men often wear a **sarong** around the waist. Somali American men usually wear Western shirts and pants instead.

Koofiyad cap: Small round cap for men.

In the United States, some young Somali American women wear Western clothes but cover their head and hair with the hijab.

Immigrants who live in Minnesota or other cold states also wear snow jackets, sweaters, boots, and gloves, which they never needed back in hot Somalia.

SERBIA

BULGARIA

MONTENEGRO

ALBANIA

GEORGIA

GR

ARMENIA AZERBAIJAN

TURKMENISTAN

YRIA

ISRAEL

JORDAN

IRAQ

I R A N

KUWAIT

EGYPT

QATAR

UNITED ARAB
EMIRATES

SAUDI
ARABIA

OMAN

ERITREA

YEMEN

SUDAN

GULF OF ADEN

DJIBOUTI

ETHIOPIA

INDIAN
OCEAN

SOMALIA

MOGADISHU

DEM. REP.
OF THE CONGO

UGANDA

KENYA

RWANDA

BURUNDI

TANZANIA

MALAWI

Somalia has the longest coastline on
the mainland of Africa. If you look closely,
the country's shape resembles the number 7.

ZAMBIA

8

ZIMBABWE

HISTORY OF SOMALIA

In ancient times, the land was called Punt. In modern times, it is the country of Somalia. Located in the Horn of Africa, in the northeast corner of the continent, Somalia curves along the coastline of the sea.

To the north of Somalia are the Gulf of Aden and the country of Yemen. To the east is the Indian Ocean. To the west and southwest are the countries of Ethiopia, Djibouti, and Kenya.

Somalia covers 246,200 square miles (396,220 km), making the country about the same size as the state of Texas. The nation had 10.8 million people as of 2016. About 2 million of them live in the capital of Mogadishu. Many Somalis in the countryside are rural **herders** and nomads, following their cattle, sheep, goats, and camels.

The nation's official language is Somali. Interestingly, Somali did not have its own alphabet until 1972. Even today, the ability to speak beautifully in poetry or stories is prized in Somali culture.

Somalia is hot, dry, and desert-like. It has had many famines and floods. In fact, people again faced starvation in 2017 when no rain fell. The difficult climate is one of the many challenges of life in Somalia.

The average life span is just 53 years for men and 55 for women. Nearly half of the population is under 15 years old because the birth rate is so high. There are nearly 6 children per woman. Child death rates are also high due to hunger and sickness.

There is also conflict in Somalia because it is in an important spot near international shipping channels. Groups keep fighting each other to control the country's resources.

INVADERS

As far back as the sixth century, invaders created ports and towns on Somalia's coastline. They sold slaves and traded goods like ostrich feathers, hides, and incense. The Muslim religion arrived with Arab settlers in the seventh century.

International forces including Americans tried to help Somali civilians escape the violence.

By the 1800s, the British, Italians, and French all invaded, fighting each other for port space and splitting up the Horn of Africa under their control. They stayed for decades.

Finally in 1960, the region gained its independence. The hopeful new country of Somalia was born. Democracy lasted nine years, and then Somalia experienced a military dictatorship. In 1991, rebels overthrew the government. In its place was no government at all. Chaos and civil war between clans and warlords wrecked the cities and rural areas. Schools closed. People went hungry. Neighboring nations of Ethiopia and Kenya and forces from the United Nations tried to make things more stable over the next decade, but their efforts were not successful.

Somali refugees live in tents made of plastic sheets in camps like Dadaab, where many families have grown to three generations.

A million Somali people fled to refugee camps to stay alive. Many tried to emigrate to the United States or other nations.

A HARD LIFE

Since about 2012, a **fragile** Somali government has operated amid hunger, sickness, danger, and corruption. Parts of northern Somalia have tried to break away. An estimated 1 million Somalis now live in African refugee camps in the countries of Kenya, Ethiopia, and Yemen or have made it to Europe or the United States. About 1 million more are refugees within Somalia itself.

Somalia's people have a vision of peace and prosperity. A new president was elected in Somalia in 2017. That inspired hope among the people who have known so much trouble. However, another bad year of **drought** meant hunger continued. The terror group Al Shabab still controlled parts of the country. Pirates continued to prey on boats in the ocean.

Somali Names

Some Somali Americans have three-part names.

Their first name is usually chosen in honor of a relative. The second name is the name of the child's father. The third name is the name of the child's **paternal** grandfather.

Somali women do not change their names when they get married. The reason for this way of naming is to keep all people identified with the father's family for life. All children in a family have the same second and third names.

Many Somali Americans only use two of their three names to make it easier to fit into daily life and the traditions of the United States.

The U.S. is home to one of the largest Somali communities outside Africa.

COMING TO AMERICA

An estimated 7 percent of all Somalis in the world now live in the United States. Most have arrived only in the last 25 years.

In the 1920s, a few Somali sailors and students came to the United States for work or school. Sixty years later in 1980, the numbers were still tiny. Only about 1,000 Somali immigrants lived in the United States.

Then, world events changed everything. When Somalia's government broke down in 1991, it created millions of refugees. At the same time, two new laws passed in the United States that made it easier for Somalis to immigrate. The Refugee Act of 1980 let more people facing **persecution** in their homeland to come to America. Another law, the Immigration Act of 1990, also made it easier for Somalis to enter.

When Somalia fell into chaos in the 1990s, hundreds of thousands of Somalis moved to big refugee camps in nearby Kenya, like Dadaab and Kakuma, to get away from the violence at home.

The Somalis thought it was temporary. They did not realize that many families would be stuck there for years with nowhere else to go.

The United States did take some of the refugees. In 1990, the United States had 2,000 Somali immigrants. By 2000, it was 36,000. By 2015, it was 90,000. Many families had children once they got here, growing the total Somali American immigrant community to nearly 150,000, by some estimates. By 2015, the vast majority of Somali refugees were coming from camps, not directly from Somalia. Most Somali Americans have settled in Minnesota and Ohio.

MINNESOTA AND MORE

Over the last 25 years, Minnesota's Somali population has grown and grown. Today it is the largest in the United States, with at least 60,000 Somali Americans. Many Somali immigrants move to Minnesota to find work. There are several factories that offer lots of jobs.

Statue of Liberty

The Statue of Liberty is a symbol of freedom and hope for all immigrants.

She was donated to the United States in 1886 by the country of France. She stands on a small island in the harbor of New York City.

In the late 1800s and early 1900s, many new immigrants sailed right past the Statue of Liberty when they arrived in America. Their hope stirred that this was the land described in the poem on the statue's pedestal: "Give me your tired, your poor, your huddled masses yearning to break free."

Today, the statue is part of a popular U.S. national park. Visitors who are in good shape can climb 377 steps to the statue's crown and look out the windows.

Made of copper with an iron scaffold interior, the statue was repaired in 1985-86 to mark the 100th anniversary of her arrival from France. Lady Liberty was an immigrant herself, and she continues to shine for immigrants today.

Somali immigrants often get their first American jobs in factories like this chicken processing plant.

Many Somalis have been able to get jobs in the meat-packing or chicken-processing factories in the Minneapolis-St. Paul area without having to speak English. Those families moved in, then others followed.

Other Somali immigrants moved to Columbus, Ohio, where an estimated 55,000 now live. Others went to Lewiston and Portland, Maine; Buffalo, New York; small towns in South Dakota; or Seattle, Washington.

Some new immigrants were somewhat dazed at their change of circumstance. For example, one Somali refugee, a young mother of two, arrived in Michigan in early 2017.

She and her daughters had been living for many years in refugee camps in Kenya and Thailand. They found life in Michigan confusing and the weather very cold. She was sometimes lonely. She was not sure if her English was good enough to get a job. Still, she felt lucky. A social service agency helped them get lodging, food, and assistance.

"In the camps, I am always thinking, when can I go to America?" she said. "Now I am here. I am happy. Here, I like so much what they do for us, respecting people. I am safe. I'm freedom. I can go everywhere."

Private agencies and local, state, and federal governments all help Somali immigrants find housing and jobs.

LIVING AS AMERICANS

In parts of Minneapolis, Minnesota, or Columbus, Ohio, there are many Somali stores, restaurants, and mosques. Schools in these cities may have a teaching assistant to help immigrant students adjust to their new school. Many Somali Americans also enjoy aspects of American culture.

One Somali American who runs an organization to help school programs in a Minneapolis suburb said moving to America comes as a shock.

"When students come to America they expect everything to be gold and that everyone lives the best life in the world. They think you just push a button and food comes to you," he told an interviewer from the Southern Minnesota Initiative Foundation in 2016. He said it comes as a surprise to students to realize there still are bills to pay and other worries, even in America.

In the Somali language, hospitality is called "martisoor." Martisoor is key to making strangers feel welcome.

LIFE IN AMERICA

The Somali American community combines parts of Somali and American culture. Here are some of the unique experiences many Somali Americans have:

★ Making friends: By living in neighborhoods where other Somalis live, new immigrants don't feel so alone. Community and social resources help them learn English, get a driver's license, get health care, and more. Schools in those neighborhoods are equipped to help Somali American children. New Somali immigrants also can bond over popular sports like soccer or meals that make them think of home. Other Somalis can help them buy a car or find a job.

Sending Remittances

Almost every Somali American immigrant sends money back to friends and relatives in Somalia or in refugee camps. Some people send money every week – and it's a lot. One estimate is that Somalis around the world send $1.4 billion back home each year! Somali Americans send an average of $3,800 per person. The money is to help people back home get enough to eat or a place to live.

Somali Americans may support their family members in Africa even if they are struggling in the United States. Family is very important in Somali culture. In Somalia, many generations of families live together. In the process of moving to a new country like the United States, many families are split up, with loved ones still waiting in camps or in a desperate situation in Somalia.

★ Food: Somali Americans may eat American food and Somali food. Lamb, goat, and beef stews, rice, beans, various flatbreads made of different grains, coffee, and tea are all staple Somali foods. Most Muslim Somali Americans do not eat pork or drink alcohol.

Many Somali Americans also like spaghetti and other Italian pastas. This Somalian tradition dates back to when Italy controlled parts of what is now the country of Somalia.

★ **Women's roles:** In Somalia, the father or oldest male relative is the head of the family. Women and men also don't mingle much unless they are related. Somali immigrants may find that the roles of husbands and wives and daughters and sons change when they move to the United States.

Many Somali women own small businesses in Minnesota and in other Somali communities. The big Karmel Square Mall in Minneapolis, for example, has hundreds of shops run by Somali women, who sell everything from clothing to food to spices to crafts. Many Somali American women also go to school and college to improve their lives.

★ **Work:** Unfortunately, many Somali American families struggle to make money. More than half of families live in poverty. The median household income in 2015 was just $23,000, with half earning more and half earning less, according to U.S. census data. That puts stress on families. The good news is that more Somali American children who are growing up in the United States speak English fluently and are going to college. Somalis have also started more than 600 businesses in Columbus, Ohio, according to the Somali Community Organization.

Many Somali immigrants see their children who are born or raised in America go on to great success.

★ Holidays: Muslim Somali Americans observe the religious period of Ramadan with a month of fasting from sunrise to sundown. At the end of Ramadan comes the happy holiday of Eid al-Fitr, with celebrations, special food, and fireworks.

★ Culture: Like other immigrant groups in the United States, many Somali Americans want to preserve their culture and language. In Minneapolis, the Somali Museum of Minnesota helps people remember what life was like in Somalia.

Ilhan Omar was elected in 2016 to represent a Minneapolis-area district in the Minnesota Legislature.

AMAZING ACHIEVEMENTS

Many Somali Americans have accomplished incredible things in many different fields. Here are some famous Somali Americans who have changed the world:

★ Ilhan Omar: She is the first Somali American to become a state representative. She serves in the Minnesota State Legislature. Born in Somalia in 1982, she grew up in a refugee camp in Kenya and moved to the United States when she was 12.

★ Mohamed Abdullahi Mohamed: This Somali American from Buffalo, N.Y., was elected president of Somalia in 2017. Born in Mogadishu, Somalia, in 1962, he came to the United States in the 1980s and graduated from the State University of New York at Buffalo. He is also the former prime minister of Somalia, serving from 2010-11. His nickname is Farmajo.

★ Abdihakem "Abdi" Abdirahman: He is a four-time Olympian representing the United

States as a track and elite marathon runner. Born in Hargeisa, Somalia, in 1977, he and his family moved to Kenya, then to the USA when he was 12. He became a U.S. citizen in 2000.

★ **Ayaan Hirsi Ali:** Activist for rights of women and girls in the Islamic world and an influential writer. Born 1969 in Mogadishu, Somalia, she moved to Kenya, then to the Netherlands in 1992. She became a member of the Dutch Parliament and made a movie about Somali women's struggles. She moved to the United States in 2007 and became a citizen in 2013.

★ **Halima Aden:** Minneapolis teen who was the first Somali American to enter a major beauty contest wearing the hijab head scarf. The Miss Minnesota USA semifinalist was then signed to a New York modeling contract. Born in a Kenyan refugee camp in 1997, she moved to the United States when she was six.

★ **Iman:** Supermodel and **philanthropist**. Born Zara Mohamed Abdulmajid in 1955 in Mogadishu, she moved to the United States for a modeling career and became a citizen. Her husband was the late British singer David Bowie.

Barkhad Abdi (left) was the first Somali American actor nominated for an Oscar. Faysal Ahmed (right) was also in *Captain Phillips*.

★ **Barkhad Abdi:** Actor. Nominated for an Academy Award as best supporting actor for his role of a pirate in the film *Captain Phillips*. He was born in 1985 in Somalia. The family moved to the country of Yemen when he was age 6, then to the United States in 1999. He is a U.S. citizen.

These are just some of the many Somali Americans who have positively impacted the United States and the world with their achievements. What amazing things will the next generation of Somali Americans accomplish?

Glossary

chaos Total lack of order.

drought Lack of rainfall.

fragile Easily broken or destroyed.

herder Person who tends sheep, goats, or cattle.

mosque Place of Muslim worship.

paternal On the father's side of a family.

persecution Causing people to suffer because of their race, religion, beliefs, or other personal factors.

philanthropist A person who donates to charities and helps others.

refugee A person who flees home seeking safety in another area or country.

sarong A loose skirt-like cloth wrapped around the body.

Sunni Muslim Branch of the Islamic religion.

For More Information

Further Reading

Gelletly, LeeAnne. *Somalia.*
New York: Simon and Schuster, 2014.

Hassig, Susan M. and Zawiah Abdul Latif. *Somalia.*
New York: Cavendish Square Publishing, 2017.

Owings, Lisa. *Somalia.*
Minneapolis, MN: Bellwether Media, 2014.

Wilson, Tammy. *Through My Eyes.*
Edina, MN: Beaver's Pond Press, 2016.

Websites

Due to the changing nature of Internet links, PowerKids Press has developed an online list of websites related to the subject of this book. This site is updated regularly. Please use this link to access the list:
www.powerkidslinks.com/cs/somaliam

Index